Messengers In Time

Tales of Antique Treasures and their Journeys Through Time

GLENN WOOD

Messengers in Time

Published in the United States of America.

ISBN:9798330289042
eISBN: 9798330307647

CONTENTS

—FORWARD—

The stories recounted here are tales told by messengers from antique lands.

They concern their creators, their owners and the travels that propelled them through time. Their tales aren't really told, they are whispered in soft voices distorted by age so that their meanings aren't always clear. Sometimes it requires a little imagination from the listener to catch the idea and fill in the gaps using experience and intuition.

The tellers have been bruised and injured along the way. They have often been nurtured and repaired further adding to their histories. All who have been shown humanity at their low points have rewarded their saviors with uplifting anecdotes from their past, gratitude for their present and the promise of contribution to a better future.

The world is so diverse but many in its history didn't know that. They were content to remain in their small communities and connect to other by travelers' tales. For most, the possibility of travel was not an option. They were routed by family, friends, crops and environment. Only great upheavals cause dislocation and the resulting journeys can be painful. Ask any border crossing refugee. But sometimes they can be positive providing a light of encouragement when before there was only the darkness of discomfort and despair.

This is a small collection of tales whispered at night by a group of these travelers who have been brought together by one who understands, values and cares for them. He, too has traveled all his life. He has seen many things, met many kindnesses along the way and appreciated that good can exist in distant places. Moreover, in foreign lands, he becomes the exotic, a fascinating entity surrounded by ears eager to hear his tales and to learn from his experiences. When experiences meld, the result is happiness and productive activity. The destination may not be clear but the approach to it, whether by foot, ship, car or plane is reward in itself. Here we try to give back a little of what has been taken. That giving is reward in itself.

The antiques that inspired these stories are palimpsests on which the hopes, joys and imaginations of the present are written….

Boxes are like people. At first glance, they are judged by their exteriors. But if what we see is sufficiently intriguing, we yearn to peek inside to see what more can be learned. It is here that the creativity and sincerity of the maker is revealed. It is here that we learn of its history, purpose and use.

The interior is the dark and mysterious yin to the exterior's yang. It is where the secrets are kept, occasionally under lock and key.

Glenn Wood, York Pennsylvania, January 2023

1.CHINA

THE MING SCHOLAR'S BOX 1631

Mr. Lin recalled the day when he ordered this box to be made. He knew it, like him, would be traveling frequently so it needed to be particularly sturdy. The main wood was jichimu, chicken wing wood, one of his favorites because it provoked in his mind many visions of birds. Although hard to the touch it presented to the eyes a vision of soft feathers. When young and recently worked the wood contains wonderful flecks of yellows, gold browns and red but the effects of age and light dim the brighter colors giving an overall appearance of a dark brown but, like a prisoner under interrogation, its identity is revealed by stress induced by strong lights.

But a box containing the two drawers he required would be very heavy if jichimu alone were used. So, the details of its construction were decided as follows. The main carcass would be of jichimu as would be the front of the drawers. This would impart a pleasing unity. All edges and corners would be strengthened with huangtong, the yellow version of the silver colored baitong that was proving popular as alternative to the silver that the Spanish were using for trade tokens. Silver was not available in China so Chinese artisans invented a mixture of metals that behaved and aged like silver. It would be another 300 years before German scientists discovered the secret of how this metal was made. Likewise, China had very little gold and so the prized mineral became jade which was reserved for exclusive use by the emperor.

By adjusting the ratio of the alloyed metals, baitong could be converted into yellow huangtong which, he judged, would nicely complement the gold flecks in the wood. In all, three different woods would be used to construct the box. In addition to the jichimu, the much lighter weight jumu, the northern elm, would form the bottoms of the two drawers. Even lighter in color and weight, the attractive satinwood would form the back and sides of the drawers. In keeping with the prevailing traditions in woodwork, the few pins required to keep the structure together would be bamboo in order not to split the wood but metal pins would be used to secure the metal parts.

As a traveling box, a lock would be needed. Unlike any western lock, its ingenious design, making use of a single hasp, would allow the two drawers to be secured to each other and to the body of the box. The only decoration permitted on the box would be the ruyi cloud pattern on the metal strengtheners. The drop pulls on the drawer fronts would be simple ellipses with only the most minute decorative perforations (for luck) which would mostly pass unnoticed. In other words, very little should detract from the beauty of the wood.

In spite of all the allowances for weight, the box required a handle at each side to facilitate lifting and securing with strings when traveling.

It was the 4th year of the ill-fated reign of Emperor Chongzhen (b.1611 - d.1644).
The invitation to travel to the northern capital, Beijing, had come from the secretary to the Chongzhen Emperor. Nobody knew it at the time but he would be the last Emperor of the Ming dynasty. In terms of the western calendar, he reigned from 1627 to 1644. "Chongzhen" meaning "honorable and auspicious" was the name he was given when he ascended to the throne at the age of 16 but Mr. Lin had known him as Zhu Youjian, when he was still a boy. He was the fifth son of Zhu Changluo, the Taichang Emperor, and one of his low-ranking concubines, Lady Liu.

When Zhu Youjian was only four years old, he learned the ugly side of palace life. His father had his mother executed and secretly buried. This left the motherless boy to be brought up by other women in the palace. This was when Lin was brought to the palace to train the boy in calligraphy, an important skill for all high-ranking officials involved in the political and cultural life of the country. These lessons were highly supervised by the palace eunuchs who had to make sure that no woman was ever present at these lessons. It was understood that it was unreasonable to require an occasional scholarly teacher to make the usual sacrifice in order to attend the palace but it was also understood that he could not spend the night in the palace hence the need to travel back and forth each day with essential equipment for the classes.

The classes continued irregularly until Zhu Youjian ascended the throne as the Chongzhen Emperor at the age of 16. Even before his enthronement, Zhu Youjian had little time for classes or relaxation as peasant rebellions became more frequent and it became more difficult to defend the northern border from attack by aggressive Manchus. They would ultimately breach the wall and arrive at Beijing in 1644 whereupon the emperor would commit suicide rather than suffer defeat and end the Ming dynasty.

As emperor, the young man found it very difficult to reign. Wars and building projects had bankrupted the country, corruption was rife and it was very difficult to find competent and trustworthy ministers to fill government posts. The emperor also tended to be suspicious of his subordinates, executing dozens of army field commanders.

It was 1631 when Lin received his invitation to visit Beijing. The imperial examinations of 1630 and 1631 marked a period of relative political calm when a new generation of scholars were appointed to high government official positions and for a brief interval, it became possible to think of artistic and cultural subjects.

But the respite was brief. In common with Europe, China was experiencing persistent drought and famine caused by the Little Ice Age. These calamities accelerated the collapse of the Ming dynasty.

Two major popular uprisings swelled up, led by men of humble origin from famine-hit Shaanxi who took up arms in the 1620s. At the same time, Ming armies were occupied in the defense of the northern border against the Manchu.

In 1631, there were rumblings of unrest and travel was an unsettling experience due to the activities of bandits occasionally attacking travelers and robbing them of valuables. Lin was enjoying his retirement by organizing the gardens surrounding his beautiful house in Suzhou. Life in Beijing had been very stressful and he was glad to be away from it. The news of palace intrigues reached even as far as distant Souzhou so he was very surprised one day to receive an invitation from the assistant to the emperor himself requesting his presence in Beijing.

The message delivered to him explained that a scroll created by Lin's grandfather had been discovered and had caught the attention of the emperor. The purpose of the visit was to appreciate the scroll and attach a personal dedication from the grandson. This was an honor which it would be unwise to decline.

Lin came from a long line of artists and calligraphers and so it was with great pride that he learned of the beautiful scroll that had been discovered in the Imperial archives bearing the seal of his grandfather. The appreciative Emperor was eager for Lin to come and add a dedication in his own hand accompanied by his own seal in red ink, as was customary.

An invitation from the emperor was really an instruction and could not be ignored even though Lin would have preferred to continue the tranquility of his retirement. Advancing years and the cessation of the demands of duty reduce the appetite for the mechanics of travel such that the desire for experiencing distant places is best carried out in the mind rather than actuality. The journey to Beijing was long and arduous even for high officials. It was likely to take a week or more and cold, hunger and general discomfort would be inevitable traveling companions.
Furthermore, it was never possible to transport all of the necessities that day-to-day life in the country required. So, the best approach was to look on the bright side and enjoy meeting his old pupil one more time. He would take some sugared persimmons as a simple gift in memory of a favored treat enjoyed by both of them.

For Lin, the most important items to accompany him on the journey were his writing instruments because these would be needed to make the appropriate dedication on the Imperial scroll. Because of the challenges involved in the journey he decided not to take his favorite writing box of huanghuali but he would use again the one made of jichimu which had served him so well in the inclement climate of Beijing. Its roomy two drawers could comfortably contain his duan stone, ink sticks, water dropper, brushes and seals of various sizes. Unlike his box made of yellow flowering pear, this one could be locked.

Jichimu is a dark understated wood in color somewhere between the light reddish brown of huanghuali and the darker purplish black of Zitan. The metal fittings that protected all of the corners and joints of the box were now somewhat corroded from the humidity and humors of the north which had a similar effect on the joints of the human body. But anyone seeing his box who had the scholar's and artist's appreciative eye would forgive any signs of damage or wear to the box itself.

Lin would travel to Beijing via the Hangzhou Grand Canal, the longest artificial river in the world and today a UNESCO world heritage site. Now, over 2000 years old, it was improved to full glory and functionality during the Ming dynasty. When the Yongle Emperor moved the Ming capital from Nanjing to Beijing in 1403, it became necessary to have good communications between the south and the north to ensure efficient supply of goods to the new capital. So, the canal was upgraded to be fully navigable for over 1000 miles of its length and up to 100m wide in parts.

The reopening of the Grand Canal also benefited Suzhou over Nanjing since the former was in a better position on the main artery of the Grand Canal, and so Suzhou became Ming China's greatest economic center. Hangzhou was located 200 km (120 mi) further down the Grand   Canal and away from the main delta. The Italian traveler Marco Polo had travelled on this canal 400 years earlier.

It was estimated that the Ming dynasty had to employ 47,000 full-time laborers in order to maintain the entire canal system. It is known that 121,500 soldiers and officers were needed simply to operate the 11,775 government grain barges in the mid-15th century.

Besides its function as a grain shipment route and major vein of river-borne indigenous trade in China, the Grand Canal had long been a government-operated courier route as well. In the Ming dynasty, official courier stations were placed at intervals of 35 to 45 km (22 to 28 miles).

The journey on the canal took a week. This cut three weeks off the journey.

On his arrival at the northern terminus of Houhai in Beijing, Lin was met by an imperial entourage to escort him to the palace. As a retired employee of the imperial court who had retained his head and other extremities, Lin was entitled to an imperial escort to the palace consisting of a stately sedan chair accompanied by a hundred servants who would take care of his belongings. Forty accompanying musicians announced his presence to passersby with drums, gongs and flutes.

The meeting with the emperor went well. Gifts were exchanged and tea was served in the pavilion of Celestial Harmony within the palace grounds. The scroll was unrolled, studied and enjoyed by the emperor and his former teacher. Lin prepared his inks for the dedication, black for the text and red for the stamp. Just as he was about to apply the moistened seal to the paper, the shrill scream of a woman broke the tranquility of the moment. Almost immediately, an official rushed into the room and begged the emperor to come quickly to the room of the second concubine. The reason was not given but Lin knew that court etiquette required him to leave immediately and not intrude on this awkward moment for the emperor.

Knowing that the formalities of a fitting farewell would be organized later, he quickly scooped up his wet brush and damp seal and unceremoniously consigned them to the drawers of his box.

Centuries would pass until an upheaval greater than the rise of the Qing. During the Cultural revolution treasures from the middle classes were appropriated by Mao's supporters. They were assumed destroyed but they were not. Porcelain, paintings, furniture, carvings all stored in vast warehouses in a form of pension fund for Mao's officers. Recently, aging revolutionaries opened the store rooms causing three, new industries to be born; the sale of stolen original Chinese antiques, the restoration and refurbishment of damaged antiques and the creation of a supply chain to sell the goods in the more gullible foreign markets.

How to tell if the box is truly old or a modern reproduction? Because wood is a natural product, it creeps with age. Ripples form on its surface which conform to the markings in the wood. In this way, they differ from undulations resulting from saw or chisel. This box, though mute, reveals its age to eye and fingertip.

Mr. Lin's box was born anew in America.

2. *RUSSIA*

THE EMPRESS BOX 1795

Catherine wasn't a detail person. She was more of a conceptual thinker interested in the 'big picture' and a visit from the British ambassador was always a source of inspiration and intellectual stimulation. As Empress of Russia, most of her days were spent receiving guests but most of them were of necessity rather than pleasure. For this particular encounter she wanted to express her appreciation of the visit with a suitable gift for the ambassador's wife - from one woman to another. That would remove any appearance of reward for services rendered in the matter of the treaty currently under negotiation. Mary, Baroness Fitzherbert had a sharp mind but politics didn't interest her. She and the ambassador, her husband Alleyne, 1st Baron St Helens had accompanied Catherine on a visit to the Crimea in 1787 and had remained friends ever since.

Unbeknownst to Catherine, the British ambassador privately derided the idea that the Russian aristocracy had really imbibed the Enlightenment culture so extravagantly propounded by the Empress, noting caustically that 'a slight though brilliant varnish' could not conceal 'illiterate and unformed minds.

Although Grigory Potemkin had ceased being her lover in 1776, her roving eye always appreciated handsome young men but it was unlikely that they would ever be invited to personal intimacy. With some enthusiasm for the project of the gift she summoned her carver- in-chief to the palace, a young artistic genius named Nikolai Stepanovitch Vereshchagin (1770
-1813). He was still in his early twenties with a shock of fair hair, piercing blue eyes and a coarse northern accent. She was sure he would understand exactly the need of the moment and express it in walrus or mammoth ivory from his native Kholmogory. He came to her attention while still in his teens owing to the refined nature of his creations and of the circle of artisans, he was inspiring in his home state of Archangelsk located in the frozen north of Russia. His most brilliant creations transformed the hard tusks of walrus into the thinnest lace-like decorations which were rapidly gaining fame as the emerging Kholmogory school.

Catherine had the connoisseur's eye for art and her agents scoured Europe for paintings and all manner of objects d'art which she used to embellish and adorn her palaces. So, when such an artistic genius emerged on Russian soil she lost no time in luring him to St Petersburg where her patronage could be more immediate. The fact that he turned out to be such a good-looking youth did nothing to frustrate his rapid ascent into the imperial circle. When he arrived in St Petersburg in 1790, he was a youth of 20; she was already 61.

Caskets in the form of a tower were popular in Moscow in the 16th century. In Kholmogory and Veliky Ustyug, they were made of wood lined with punched iron, which turned such items into a kind of safes. Bone caskets of this type were often made to order. These were expensive products that were supplied to the palaces of Russian tsars and nobility.

It was decided that a sewing box would be the ideal gift. Owing to the short notification time, it would be made in Nikolai's workshop in St Petersburg, an upgraded version of the one founded by Peter the Great a century earlier. It would be of strict classical form with rectangular base and a drawer. Time didn't allow for a fully carved top surface so a small painting of the ferry crossing wharf at Kholmogory would be substituted.

Kholmogory was a village, port and administrative center in the Arkhangelsk oblast (region) of northwestern European Russia. It lies along the Northern Dvina River 47 miles (75 km) southeast of the city of Arkhangelsk. The village has existed since 1355, when it served traders as a riverine port enroute to the White Sea. It grew into a large commercial center in the 15th and 16th centuries.

The entire surface of the box is covered with carved ornaments and plates with foil backing. The high quality of the work, the superbly developed style allows us to say with confidence that this artistic creation was made on special order by the outstanding master of bone carving N.S. Vereshchagin who often came from Arkhangelsk to St. Petersburg and carried out orders for the Imperial Court.

On our box, the repeat consists of four repeating elements rather than the more usual two. See diagram below.

At a glance, it appears that the scrolling element with a flower at the center is the repeating element but this is not the case.

The complete design is symmetrical about the central vertical. The snake-like elements separating flowers one and two and three and four can be seen to be mirror images of each other. Also, no two adjacent scrolls surrounding the flowers turn in the same direction. They alternate between clockwise and anticlockwise. In other words, adjacent webs scroll in opposite directions. Simplicity didn't figure in Nikolai's vocabulary. He worked for his own satisfaction, not that of others.

The hardness of an elephant's tusks registers approximately 2.75-3.50 on the Mohs scale. The working process of all ivory is performed with chip removal. The grain must be noted at all times in this procedure. It is also vital that the material is not overheated. Working against the grain leads to the surface being torn. Splintering occurs, which can only be rectified with the removal of relatively thick layers of ivory. The poor thermal conductivity of ivory means that special care should be taken when using rotating tools and machines as this can cause overheating. However, mammoth ivory is one of the hardest materials in this range (Mohs hardness 3-5). Consequently, here it is possible to work very precisely, even with very small dimensions, without the material breaking.

Mary was thrilled to receive the sewing box but never used it for sewing purposes. Although much admired and appreciated when she returned to England it became a plaything for children, hers and those of future generations. Although never abused, childish handling took its toll on the delicate carving so when it arrived at an auction saleroom in London in 2022, it was a shadow of its former self. Worse, it wasn't even recognized for the treasure it was. At least it escaped the ignominy of being described as the work of a Napoleonic POW, a common fate of Russian bone boxes. It was correctly described as 'a late 18th/early 19thC Russian bone veneered box similar to others produced in Archangel / Archangelsk. '

Its shabby appearance allowed a collector to acquire it for a modest outlay, ship it to America and undertake a long and painstaking restoration bringing it back to its former glory.

Boxes by the same maker appear on the front covers
of two books published about Vereshchagin and his artistry.

Box with comparable printed on the front cover of Russian book.

Although it cannot compete with the two Vereshchagin vases gifted to the American Ambassador and now housed in the Metropolitan Museum of Art in New York, at least America can claim three pieces by this most distinguished of makers and the only one whose illustrious twin graces the cover of the only book dedicated to historical Russian carved ivory.

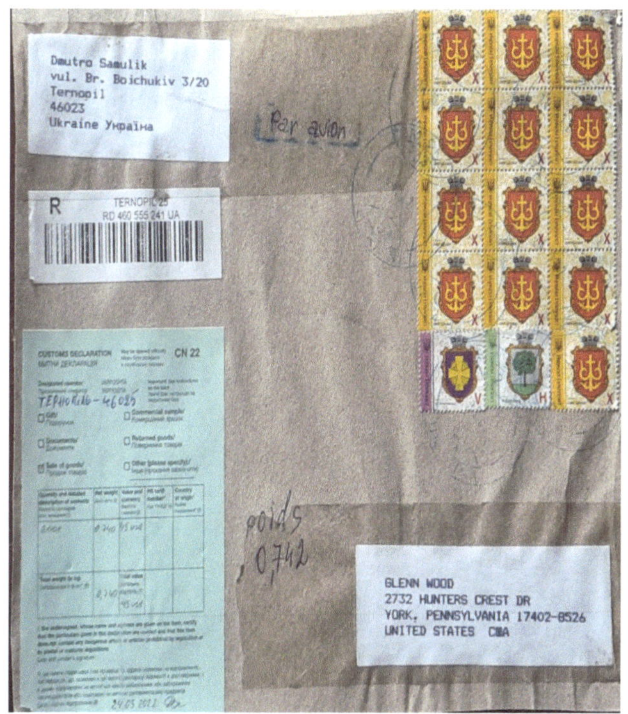

Written by I.N. Ukhanova (The curator of the Hermitage's department of decorative art) the book is only available in Russian.

Title: 'Reznaia kost'. Tvoreniia russkikh masterov XVIII- XIX vekov iz sobraniia sem'i Karisalovykh / 'Carved Ivory': works by Russian artists of the 18th and 19th c. from the Karisalovys' collection)

In a poignant coda to history, this author's copy was imported from Ukraine a month following the Russian invasion in 2022. Ukrainian bookseller Dmitro Samulik shipped the book from Ternopil to Kiev in the package pictured. It traveled by train to Krakow, Poland thence to Warsaw where it eventually boarded a flight to New York.

3.ENGLAND

SIR CHRISTOPHER'S LACE BOX 1690

Nobody needs a lace box these days. One might come in handy for the storage of jewelry, writing equipment or other odds and ends but, in our digital age, even writing necessities have become as superfluous as lace collars and kerchiefs. But 'need' isn't 'wanted' so if anyone would like to possess one, it should be this.

It has long grain banding around the top and frieze. This transports us to the period centered on the year 1690, maybe a little earlier but not much later. The gorgeous figured walnut used is saw cut veneer. The top is veneered with quarter panels of figured walnut. It is further inlaid with herringbone borders and cross banding. The top also has a cross grain molded edge. The front and the sides display mirrored panels of walnut veneer and herringbone borders. There is a cross grain cavetto base molding around the bottom edge. This spectacular wood anchors us in the 'age of walnut'. This period in English decorative woodwork slots neatly between the Tudor 'age of oak' and the Georgian 'age of mahogany'.

It has an early mercury gilt escutcheon in front of the original iron lock and original lock pin, just as Sir Christopher specified originally. The old hinges are secured with rose head nails and the original baseboard is covered with felt. The interior has been lined with silver paper. The rear of the box is not veneered and was stained to emulate walnut. The dovetailed construction is apparent.

Oak is a splendid wood for many applications but it is open grained and does not lend itself to fine carving or decorative effects. On the other hand, England had to wait until the 18thC for mahogany to become available from Africa or the West indies. So, it was a bone to English furniture that William & Mary (reigned 1688 - 1702) popularized the use of European walnut thus making the wait tolerable.

Walnut trees are not native to England. They were introduced by the Romans who used them for their nuts and oil. By the Middle Ages, the trees were almost extinct and walnut was considered an exotic timber. As there was only a limited supply of walnut in Britain, much of the timber had to be imported. France was an important source for the timber, Juglans regia, between 1680 and 1720 so our box was most likely enrobed in veneer from that source. A severe winter in 1709 destroyed a great number of the trees in central Europe, which led to the French prohibition of walnut exportation in 1720. This abrupt halt in trade had serious implications for the walnut trade in England and ushered in the mahogany age.

One critical aspect of any box intended to store delicate clothing accessories like lace was the smoothness of the interior. Any snagging would be prejudicial to the appearance of the precious contents. Often, they were lined with silk or other fine cloth but Sir Christopher Make piece's involvement in the tea trade was suggesting an alternative. Having made his fortune in the cultivation and sale of saffron, he was intrigued by the emerging interest in dried tea leaves. Tea had reached Britain by the 1660s and was rapidly becoming an expensive but fashionable luxury product. Polite circles such as his own consumed it at least once a week and stored the dry leaves in lockable containers as protection from theft or adulteration by the domestic staff. Indeed, most things had to be protected from thieving fingers which is why he specified a working lock for the lace box he just ordered. His tea was imported by the British East India Company but he had already made his first shipment directly from China.

The crates into which the tea was packed were traditionally lined with thin metal. His packers in China had recently developed a method of rendering paper impervious to moisture by fortifying with a very thin layer of metal. This cost reducing development gave the Chinese a slight edge over India whose product tended to spoil somewhat in the long sea journey to England which could take up to a year. He didn't know what, exactly, was this metal/paper material but he had the idea to harvest some from one of his tea chests and use it to line his lace box. Tea packing in China showing cases lined with metal paper.

Tea Packing in China showing cases lined with metal paper

Sir Christopher didn't own much lace He wasn't what might be called today a snappy dresser. As a Protestant he was less dogmatic than the Puritans who were taking root in East Anglia but he resented the residual fashion for exaggerated dress and insistence on ceremonies so beloved by Catholics. He considered these things as useless as the papal pudenda. He welcomed the accession to the throne of William and Mary in 1688 because King James 11 had become overly sympathetic to Catholics and Catholicism. The preceding year James passed the Declaration of Indulgence Act which removed all laws restricting the rights of Catholics. The subsequent arrest of Bishops who opposed the Act lead the people of England to search for a new leader in fear of a Catholic monarchy. It wasn't the attachment to exotic costumes and rituals that irked him, it was the implicit requirement for a suspension of common sense and the ability to reason.

The Enlightenment, begun in Italy in the 15thC showed people that it was possible to question things and that an answer could be found that didn't involve magic, demons or divine control. He had once attended a Catholic mass and found the pomp and ceremony of it overwhelming. He felt that in another time and place the priests would be decked in feathers and bright paints chanting invocations whose meaning was incomprehensible to the majority of people. Latin was equally obscure to all but the educated elites. London had been devastated by fire in 1666 which had quickly followed a disastrous plague the year before and maybe it was true that all these ills were divine retribution for something although there was no agreement as to what exactly was being punished.

The relative isolation of his lodge high on the hill in Saffron Walden ensured he escaped the worst of those misfortunes but he was very sure that personal endeavor, creativity and enterprise were leading the country to new found comfort and wealth rather than any act of the divine. He couldn't accept that his personal success was the result of deep and sustained prayer or the will of the Almighty. Neither was entry into Heaven the result of divine selection. His Protestant faith indicated to him that everyone's path is determined by their own endeavors and that hard work, rather than prayer, leads to ultimate salvation.

So, when Anne, the youngest daughter of King James 11 was crowned Queen in 1702, Sir Christopher felt energized to pursue expansive business ventures. Although Anne's father had been a Catholic, she detested Roman Catholics and Dissenters and had a will that promised a new expansionist golden age to be blessed with military victories abroad and the creation of wealth for the generations.

He still needed to travel to London from time to time and for these trips, attention had to be paid to dress and appearance. For those occasions, what few elegant accessories he possessed went with him. Those were the norms of the society in which he moved. It was prudent to respect them but his careful frugality urged investment in his next shipment rather than an expansion of his wardrobe. It pleased him that his fellow merchants shared his values and derived pleasure from arguing about the merits of the spice trade and how it might be exploited to mutual benefit rather than pontificating about the divine right of kings.

The box which contained his lace cuffs, collars and kerchiefs also acted as the protector of his precious copy of the bible. The greatest achievement of Anne's great grandfather James1 had been the commissioning of the translation of this bible from the Hebrew and Greek into clear and comprehensible English. This text had been a great comfort to him and source of inspiration on his travels and gave him pride that he didn't have to endure the 'mumbo jumbo' of the Latin mass of which the Roman priesthood was so enamored. With the passage of time, his laces wore out and were not replaced. His precious bible became the sole occupant of the box.

He would have found it a rich irony that, like his Puritan neighbors, the box eventually found its way to Massachusetts. It now resides in Pennsylvania, a commonwealth founded by his fellow student at Oxford, William Penn where it currently offers accommodation to a laptop, tablet, cell phone and remote; a highly adaptable survivor that, unlike the lace, never went out of fashion.

4.INDIA

25

PROF. EMBREE'S MONGHYR BOX 1901

Kali Charan was well known to British travelers in Victorian India. With his jaunty turban and twittering English, he had an innate ability to charm because he could see into the soul of his audience. His shop or 'emporium' as he liked to call it, was often frequented by English travelers commuting between India's two major cities, namely Calcutta and Delhi. Although Delhi would not become India's capital until the British built New Delhi and handed it over in 1947, there was a great deal of toing and froing throughout the time of the Raj. Apparently, Mr. Charan was distantly related to Mansur Ali Khan, the Nawab of Bengal who had abdicated in 1880, but so were many people given that the Nawab had 39 children in his short 59-year life.

Monghyr, neatly situated on a curve of the Ganges River between Calcutta, near the coast, and Delhi as far inland as it was possible to be in India. Mr. Charan, as he was generally known, also claimed a vague association with the East India Company. His engaging conversation was always peppered with references to Clive of India and Warren Hastings whose wife had been served by Mr. Charan's family when she convalesced in the Monghyr fort overlooking the river.

Mr. Charan knew well that relationship building with clients was essential; it was a necessary precu0rsor to sales. Win their affection and orders will follow. Purchases were generally a long-term affair with Mr. Charan because although he had plenty of boxes, cabinets and desk furniture on show in his shop, most clients preferred to order something customized to their needs which they would collect the next time they were passing through. For those who can afford it, there is a natural inclination to prefer the bespoke to the regular. A premium is readily paid for the luxury of the unique. When travel up the river was by boat, there was usually enough time during the layover at Monghyr to have his craftsmen fulfil the order within a day or so but after the railway was built by the British to by-pass the town in 1862, the pace of the traveler's life had quickened but that of his workers had not.

As time went on, the work of inlaying all those small ivory pieces proved too time consuming and Mr. Charan felt that some variation was necessary to shorten the lead time and present a more robust and masculine aesthetic to the piece. Even though many of the ultimate recipients of his work might be ladies, the buyers were almost always men. They lived in a man's world of diplomacy, commerce or the military and they were the ones who controlled the purse strings.

After a few tests, the pattern with a grouping of three ivory circles, one larger than the other two and containing a cryptic symbol lifted from the Vedas, proved most appealing. In 1901, two things happened which would have a short but noticeable effect on this decoration. Firstly, Queen Victoria died and her passing had a profound effect on those who served in her favorite colony and secondly, he received an invitation to exhibit some pieces in the Delhi Exhibition to be held in 1903.

One of his friends and occasional customer was Mr. George Watt who traveled extensively in India often accompanied by his young and charming assistant Percy Brown. On one of these visits, Mr. Watt had confided that there was to be a huge exhibition in Delhi towards the end of 1902 and its purpose was to promote the arts and crafts of India. Mr. Watt was to prepare the catalogue and organize the collection of the exhibits along with Mr. Brown and that if anything special required prepayment, Mr. Watt was in a position to arrange that. This was an opportunity Mr. Charan could not miss. And so it was that he hired one of the ebony workers from Nagina to introduce a new decorative technique to his Manghir wares. That's how a simple but effective background was "borrowed" from Nagina ebony work to produce an effect that had not been previously seen in Monghyr.

The final catalogue entry in Mr. Watt's catalogue would describe the effect as follows:

'The pattern of ornamentation was formerly a minute spray and flowers in stiff conventionalism.

Recently the inlayers seem to have got a new conception. They turn out cabinets, card tables and other such articles in response to the universal model demand for articles of quasi-European household furnishing. The style of ornamentation has also changed and perhaps improved though it is difficult to form an opinion as to the origin of the design or its possible future developments. Three circular pieces of Ivory, one larger than the other two, are inlaid at fixed intervals, while the interspaces and ebony are incised and punched, thus giving an effective background to the diaper of ivory.'

The construction of the vast exhibition was to begin in May 1902 with a view to a grand opening in December later that year. That didn't leave much time to assemble his final collection of items for the part of the exhibition that he would share with representatives of other parts of India. It had to be admitted that his craftsmen were not great carvers. Their skills were mostly developed in the local factory which made rifles and other firearms for which Munghyr was justifiably famous but elaborate carving wasn't a requirement for these articles whereas inlaying rifle stocks was a useful decorative skill. Therefore, he decided it would be best to share the section of the exhibition concerned with inlay work in wood.

There are several centers in India which have excelled in inlay work for generations and the styles can instantly be recognized by those experience in the art. Inlay may be accomplished by metals, ivory, bone, mother-of-pearl or by other woods. When using metal either large pieces can be used or fine wire, the former becomes the kind of encrusting and the latter a form of Damascening.

So he would share his booth area with representatives of the chief Indian centers of inlaying such as Hoshiarpur where ivory or bone and also brass are inlaid on sheesham (aka Indian rosewood), Chiniot where brass alone is used and Mainpuri where copper and brass wires are both used. He would represent Munghyr of Bengal showing skills of ivory inlay. Nepal, also a part of the British Empire, would also be invited to show its work inlaying ivory but using blackwood as a base owing to the difficulty in obtaining the lustrous and dense ebony available in Munghyr.

It was with slight irritation that Mr. Charan learned that exhibits from Mysore would be included in the same inlayers section. His Highness the Maharaja of that state had given great encouragement to the inlayers of that area by commissioning them to create doors and articles of furniture for his new palace. Mysore is most famous for its sandalwood carving but this would be represented in a separate division.

All works of art are the result of an iterative process meaning that they do not materialize fully fledged but are the result of repeated observation and modification. In a sense, a first draft is created, and after critical scrutiny, is improved. This process may be often repeated until a satisfying result is achieved. It is a consequence of the conscious part of the brain allowing time for the subconscious to pursue its deliberations quietly without interruptions. Geniuses such as Mozart do not produce a first draft. They go straight to the finished version but the brain is still working in the same way. In that case, input from the eye or ear is provided by the imagination. In this realization, any input from an audience is completely excluded from this process. But in Mr. Charan's case, he had the special advantage of repeat customers over many years who had commented on his output whereupon he was able to convey the constructive criticism and feedback to his talented workers.

As Mr. Charan would be the sole exhibitor from Munghyr he was not afraid of competition from other producers in Bengal but he was keen to use his display to both enhance his reputation and also capitalize on the event. He planned to submit a cabinet, a card table, a tea table and a couple of work boxes, one of which would display the new decorative effect he had in mind. Its reception would provide useful feedback on whether this technical development would be worth pursuing or not. Mr. Charan sensed that the world was now craving innovation - for new things, experiences and sensations. But these desires are always counterbalanced by the comforting reassurance of tradition. Tradition represents continuity and safety. It is pre- approved and isn't subject to the vagaries of novelty which can provide short term reward but also bankruptcy for those who invest too heavily in it.

So, Mr. Charan felt that he had chosen his exhibition pieces wisely representing, as they did, old favorites which had proved their popularity and resilience in the past with just enough innovation to excite informed comment. Only lack of comment or interest could be construed as useless as it provided no direction.

The day finally arrived and Mr. Charan was able to attend the opening speech by Lord Curzon on 30th December 1902 which began with the words:

'If Indian arts and handicrafts are to be kept alive, it can never be by outside patronage alone. I should like to see a movement spring up amongst the Indian chiefs and nobility for the expurgation or, at any rate, the purification of modern tastes, and for a reversion to the old- fashioned but exquisite styles and patterns of their own country.'

He wasn't quite sure what it meant because his own business was totally reliant on 'outside patronage' but at least the 'exquisite styles and patterns' of his country were favorably mentioned although when juxtaposed with the term 'old fashioned' the praise seemed somewhat diluted.

One of the first visitors to his booth was Major Morrison who was already a good customer and had purchased a couple of pieces previously. He greatly appreciated the density and blackness of the ebony that Mr. Charan always incorporated into his pieces. The first piece the Major purchased in 1875 was a miniature cabinet decorated in typical style with hundreds of small ivory pieces representing flower sprays and scrolling tendrils.

The doors of a cabinet conveniently decorated with the leaves and fruit of Diospyros monoxylon, the ebony tree from which these Monghyr items are made.

Ainslie T. Embree (1921 - 2017)

Ainslie T. Embree was Professor of History (1958-1991) and Professor Emeritus of History (1991-2017), Columbia University.

The doors were decorated with the leaves and fruit of the ebony tree used in the construction of the piece. In time, the wood would simply be known as 'ebony' but few trees yield such a uniformly black and fine-grained wood as diospyros monoxylon.

The Major was so taken with the new design that he quickly decided to purchase two boxes, one showing the older style and the other demonstrating the fresh, more severe new style developed for the exhibition.

OLD STYLE

NEW STYLE

DECORATION DETAIL

Both boxes traveled back to the home counties in England with Major Morrison's luggage. The old style one remained in England until 2022 when it was acquired at auction by the present owner and shipped to USA.

The new style one crossed the Atlantic decades earlier to expand the collection of America's leading authority on India.

Professor Ainslie Embree was a historian, cultural ambassador and a leading scholar of modern Indian history. He was instrumental in introducing South Asian studies into US College curricula. It is believed he acquired the box when serving as a fellow of Saint Antony's College of the University of Oxford in England.

His personal signed copy of 'Indian Art at Delhi 1903' by George Watt is also owned by the present author and has served as a guide in writing this essay.

5. FRANCE

THE BAGARD BOX 1690

In 1689, French laws made it illegal to manufacture luxury items from precious metals, because silver was needed to pay for Louis XIV's foreign wars. His vast military campaigns resulted in the setting up of the sumptuary decrees of 1689-1709. These required that small personal items, such as toiletries, boxes and mirrors could no longer be silver or gold. To imitate Louis XIV, who had melted his objects in gold and silver, the upper classes sought a substitute for these precious metals.

The carvers of Nancy in the independent Duchy of Lorraine (now in eastern France) subsequently made a great success of carved versions of such pieces using fruit woods such as pear and very fine-grained cherry wood known in French as bois de Sainte-Lucie. Both the forms and the decoration were based on contemporary silverware. The trade continued until at least the 1740s.

The importance of Nancy as a center of sculpture in Europe cannot be overstated. It was dominated by the Bagard family, a dynasty of three famous sculptors in Nancy. These sculptors were active from the end of the 16th century to the beginning of the 18th century. They were Nicolas Bagard, his son César and finally Toussaint. The best known is César Bagard (1620 - 1709). Born in Nancy in 1620, he was a pupil of the great Jacquin, known as the best sculptor in Lorraine of his time. His expertise was so appreciated that he also earned the nickname "Grand Caesar". He worked for many personalities in France including the Duke of Lorraine. Also in Paris on the triumphal arch erected on the occasion of the marriage of Louis XIV.

César Bagard created boxes, cupboards, and wooden utensils using Bois de Sainte-Lucie. The Nancy craftsmen made these Sainte Lucie wooden articles using the repertoire of patterns found on objects made of precious metal. Less precious and less fragile than lacquer, the Sainte Lucie wood lends itself perfectly to the delicate workmanship of the goldsmith.

Indirectly, this Sainte Lucie tree established Lorraine and the city of Nancy as a center of excellence for sculpture. In order to cope with the demand for his wood carvings, César Bagard expanded his workshop and took on Jacob Sigisbert Adam as an apprentice. Subsequently, the sculptor Jacob Sigisbert Adam (1670 - 1747), rose to become a renowned representative of French late baroque and a virtuoso master in small format sculpting.

In 1699, Jacob Sigisbert Adam began to execute commissions for Leopold, Duke of Lorraine. Nowadays a charming centerpiece made for the court of Nancy from 1701, showing Cupid amidst frogs, is still preserved. A year later he made small animal sculptures (a deer and eight dogs), intended as decoration for the duke's banquets. In 1724 he also made the figures of the nativity scene for the ducal Christmas festivities. In addition to such small pieces, Jacob Sigisbert Adam also executed large works, such as a lead sculpture for the park of the Lunéville palace.

However, his small sculptures in bronze and terracotta made the largest contributions to his fame but his three sons would go on to work on the outdoor sculptures at Versailles.

The Sainte Lucie tree is a wild cherry and has an exotic history. It belongs to a genus where most, if not all members produce hydrogen cyanide, a poison that gives almonds their characteristic flavor. This toxin is found mainly in the leaves and seed and is readily detected by its bitter taste. It is usually present in too small a quantity to do any harm but any very bitter seed or fruit should not be eaten. In small quantities, hydrogen cyanide has been shown to stimulate respiration and improve digestion. It is also claimed to be of benefit in the treatment of cancer. In excess, however, it can cause respiratory failure and even death.

The tree and its fruits have been known and appreciated from antiquity. It has the unusual botanical name of Prunus mahaleb and is a likely candidate for the ḫalub-tree mentioned in early Sumerian writings, a durable fruit-bearing hardwood with seeds and leaves known for their medicinal properties and associated with the goddess Innana, an ancient Mesopotamian goddess of love, war, and fertility. She is also associated with beauty and divine justice. She was worshiped in Sumer and later by the Babylonians and Assyrians under the name Ishtar.

The Arabic mahleb or mahlab meaning the mahaleb cherry appears in medieval Islamic writings. Ibn Al-Awwam in his book on agriculture dated to the late 12th century described how to cultivate the mahaleb tree: he says the tree is a vigorous grower, easy to grow, but is not resistant to prolonged drought. He also described how to prepare the mahaleb seeds by boiling them in sugared water. One early record in Latin appears in 1317 in an encyclopedia by Matthaeus Silvaticus who wrote that the "mahaleb" is the kernel seed of the fruit of both domesticated and wild cherry trees in Arabic countries. Today its cultivation and use is largely restricted to the former Ottoman Empire with Syria being is the main exporting country. From its early roots in modern Iraq, the tree made its way up to North Africa crossing into Europe from Morocco to Spain and thence to France.

This particular box celebrates the very tree from which it is made. It draws inspiration from the floral kingdom and highlights some large bloomed peonies in a basket of flowers. But close examination reveals small sprays of the five petalled St Lucy flowers which also appear in the strapwork cartouche surrounding the flower basket.

When discovered in London in 2022, this box had already suffered at the hands of an unsympathetic restorer who had not only coated all the exterior with a dark varnish (probably to disguise the shrinkage crack in the lid) but had also carried out thoughtless repairs to the interior.

There is a similar box in the Metropolitan Museum in New York which still hides under an unflattering layer of varnish. Very careful removal of this varnish, carried out over dozens of hours under a strong light and magnifiers, finally revealed the original exquisitely detailed carving defining all the flowers and leaves that can finally be appreciated once again.

Another unexpected consequence of restoration to the interior was the discovery of the original hinges completely covered previously with wood additions aimed at strengthening the hinges and box walls. A more recent desecration was the lining of the box with a faux leather, plastic lining presumably intended to render the box more saleable when it came to auction in 2022.

Before and During Restoration.

The modern plastic lining was removed, the glue cleaned and the original hinges revealed and restored. Screws and round shanked nails didn't become available until the industrial revolution in the 18thC. The only pins and nails used on this box were square in cross section so the screws used at some point to secure the hinges were replaced with age-appropriate nails.

The luxurious originals in precious metals are long gone whereas their humbler equivalents in wood remain. Glory and celebrity are often fleeting.

Modesty can occasionally be a better survival strategy.

6.ITALY

THE RENAISSANCE BOX 1631

Few things focus the mind like the threat of torture or death. Usually, it is the relentless march of years that causes the brain to dwell increasingly on the value of time and its true nature as a diminishing resource. But occasionally, circumstances force a similar appreciation at an earlier age. At this moment Giorgio's mind was fully focused in the freezing dark dungeon in which he found himself. Lit by only a single candle it was difficult to see the few things that surrounded him and made his wretched life more tolerable. As the grandson of Federico III da Montefeltro (1422 – 1482) he had a right to expect a few more creature comforts while he awaited his fate. But even when enshrined in law, rights are not always counterbalanced by duties. As a high-ranking member of a noble family, it was reasonable to expect more respect than might be afforded to a member of the lower classes but Brescia in the 16thC was a rough neighborhood.

The power struggles in Lombardy involving the aristocracies of Milan and Verona coupled with the meddling interference of the French caused ferocious instability and at this precise moment Giorgio found himself on the losing side of an ego clash. Of course, the charges brought against him were trumped up but, in an age of enlightenment and truth, the candle of intrigue, deception and subterfuge had not been extinguished. Indeed, the recently published writings of Niccolò Machiavelli were as widely discussed in noble circles as the bible and the idea of 'ends justifying the means' expounded in 'The Prince' were highly attractive to power grabbers.

Suddenly, the incandescence of an idea warmed him. It was audacious and devious and there was a strong possibility it wouldn't work but, in this situation, anything was worth a try. To enact the plan, he needed one of his old writing boxes. Under the pretext that he would prepare a confession, his jailer was dispatched to his office in the Palazzo Ducale di Gubbio to collect all that he would need in order to prepare this document signed and authenticated with his personal seal.

This personal writing casket contained a secret essential to the functioning of his plan. The casket had been made in the Minelli family workshop. It had gained enormous prestige for their development of the art of intarsia, a technique of inlaid wood artfully and decoratively inlaid to look like painting. This type of woodworking dated back to the 13th century and was becoming very popular in Renaissance Italy. The technique eventually arrived to decorate the cathedrals of Europe. It traveled via Andalusia and Sicily from the mosques and minarets of North Africa, where, due to the prohibition on graven images, it was useful in effecting complex calligraphic patterns and geometrical designs.

The skill of the Minelli family lay in carving out recesses in walnut wood and filling them with other woods exactly cut to fit the prepared space. Not only were different woods used for the inlay to enhance the realism of the design but they were a family skilled in mathematics and numerology which they incorporated into all their work. The dimensions of Giorgio's box were based on the golden ratio and the same proportional relationship, in association with the series of Leonardo Fibonacci, was contained in the scroll of the supporting feet, a visually pleasing shape adopted by the violin makers of Cremona and Brescia as graceful scrolls to finish the peg boxes of their instruments rather than cherubs. It also harbored other secrets only apparent to the learned cognoscenti.

For example, the lid construction would not normally be visible from the inside which would be covered but during restoration it became apparent the normal frame and panel construction system was not used.

The apparent 'inserts' in the four corners belong to the upper and lower stretchers because the side stretchers are lap dovetailed into the upper and lower struts. Ink stains appear where the two ink wells would have originally been positioned in their respective compartments below.

The box, together with some sheets of fresh parchment, ink and his seal were duly brought and balanced on the shaky table that supported his candle.

While he made a pretense of drafting first one and then another 'confession' he asked that the box be returned directly to his sister in the family home.

A small bribe to the jailer ensured that this was done but two days later, tired of waiting for his written confessions, the committee appointed to consider his case found him guilty and he was summarily executed the next day. Unlike today when judicial procedures against the wealthy and well connected can take months or years, in most places throughout history judgement has been swift and brutal.

His sister was distraught not only on account of the loss of her sibling but it also meant that the family property and wealth would be seized. It was ironic that her family's success had been based on the recruitment, training and deployment of mercenaries but they were always away fighting and not available to protect the family's direct interests at short notice. Apart from the loss of her brother, the stripping away of the luxuries afforded by the family's position would be particularly hard to endure.

There was no shortage of gold in the family vaults but wealth and luxury need to be deployed with wisdom and cunning if the comfort and prestige of the owner are to be maintained.

In the context of wealth, gold has symbolized authority and power for millennia. The churches and cathedrals of northern Europe have used it in industrial quantities to impress the impressionable. It has many properties causing it to be prized. Historically these were scarcity, malleability (the ability to be beaten into thin sheets), ductility (the ability to be drawn into fine wires), and of course, freedom from oxidation. More recently, its high electrical conductivity has been added to its intrinsic properties but all these properties only support luxury when a craftsman has labored skillfully and lengthily to convert it into an object of beauty. As Dr Johnson observed 'the finest statue carved from a carrot elicits curiosity but not admiration'. More challenging materials should be used such as jade, ivory, stones and metals. The stored value of labored hours adds to the satisfaction of possession. The rarer the better to convey the idea of 'luxury' to the owner.

Gold and other precious metals have fulfilled this role from ancient times but only when it is fashioned into something wonderful is its value fully appreciated. Some materials hardly require such elaboration because they have inherent fascination. These are the optically active materials that play games with normal light causing it to dance and sparkle. Glass can do this but diamonds and gemstones do it better. Iridescent pearls, too, harness light to fascinate and entrance.

The inner workings of the original medieval lock

Giorgio had several writing boxes and it remained a mystery to Donatella why her brother had insisted on this one. It's true it bore the family crest and the fleur de lis symbol of Florence and Tuscany but it had become shabby through use and Giorgio had other, finer ones with more reliable locks.

It would be 400 years later that a collector of antique boxes would notice that the depth of the interior of the box didn't exactly match the external depth. After some internal inspection and adjustments, a very shallow secret side drawer would be revealed in which a single sheet of hand written parchment would be found. On it, in shaky handwriting, were instructions to entrust a huge bribe to a family friend who had connections with Giorgio's adjudicating committee. In this world of dog eat dog, Giorgio knew that everything could be secured for the right price. It was only a question of fitting the price to the weak link and, if that could be secured, like snugly associating the correct key to its lock, his life might be spared.

The plan was a good one and for half the family gold bullion his life would be saved but the sad flaw was that his sister had forgotten about the secret drawer even assuming that she ever knew about it. So often in life we disclose secrets in the knowledge and expectation that they will be shared. There is no value to a secret that is unknown. The suicide's cry for help has no value if it falls onto deaf ears or no ears at all.

Only lies travel faster than secrets. When even nuclear secrets can be misappropriated and stored in a janitor's closet, it becomes clear that the objective is not the non-disseminations of the contents. What distinguishes being told a secret from simply receiving some information is that the annotation 'secret' is a categorical imperative adding deliciousness and perceived value to the information contained. There is an implied exclusivity and that is intoxicating. And exclusivity is the basis of luxury.

Giorgio's intrigue was ultimately responsible for his downfall.

7. BURMA

THE QUEEN'S JEWEL BOX 1880

The year was 1878 and Heinrich Kaufmann was brooding in his office in Solingen, Germany. Solingen had been famous for its high-quality steel since the Middle Ages and was particularly well known for its blades in knives and swords.

Herr Kaufmann had started his business in the manufacturing of steel goods in 1856 and had enjoyed immediate success with sales in and around Germany. But he was a man of ambition and vision and was casting his eyes to the lucrative markets opening up in the Far East. He had already appointed an agent in Bombay who was proving very successful in finding niche markets in British India. So much so that he was planning an expanded factory in Germany called India Werke and had already contracted an engineering company to design it.

His current factory would be relocated to 55 Hochstrasse and represented a huge investment on him personally and his family but he was confident that further expansion into Asia would result in the need for a significant increase in his production capacity. He already had agents in Manila, Bangkok, Singapore, and Jakarta who were not only indicating customer interest in his products but were sending orders which he was struggling to fulfil.

Thailand in particular was showing great promise causing him muse over the potential of the adjacent country of Burma and its capital of Mandalay.

News had reached him of the death of the much-loved King Mindon and accession to the throne by his son Thibaw. Mindon's son by a lesser queen, succeeded him after his death in 1878.

Mindon had a prolific personal breeding program siring 110 children with his 62 queens so succession was never going to be a simple matter.

The political situation was unstable and Mindon had spent much of his reign fighting off the British who were constantly attempting to expand their empire beyond the Indian subcontinent. Poor Thibaw didn't know it but he would be the last king of Burma before being ousted by the British in 1885 and exiled to India.

The German ambassador had detected a resentment on the part of King Thibaw towards the British which could favor Kaufmann's ambitious plans. He felt that business prospects could be very good if only he could find the right way to introduce himself and his company into that country. Success in business depends less on what you are selling and more of the strength of the network you have formed. In situations like this, knowledge is power.

It was known that Thibaw had studied (1875–77) in a Buddhist monastery and had a somewhat gentle nature but, as king, he was strongly influenced by his wife, Supayalat, and her mother.

His accession to the throne was accompanied by much violence and civil strife caused by sibling rivalry but his route to success lay though his scheming and manipulative mother-in-law. She invited all other claimants to the throne to come to the Royal palace to attend the king's deathbed. On arrival they were summarily executed and buried in the palace grounds. Thibaw was quickly enthroned at a cost of 70 dead princes and princesses killed by one of their own.

Heinrich sought the opinion of his son who had already made a visit to India and was becoming more involved in the business following his graduation from the University of Heidelburg.

Between them they hashed out a plan to make a gift to King Thibaw of a bejeweled box in the fashionable Mandalay style. The box would contain a written introduction to the Kaufmann company, endorsed by the German ambassador, recommending the company as a reputable supplier of arms, especially knives and swords which could be supplied to Thibaw's army under favorable terms.

Heinrich's son Ulrich, known to family and friends as Uli, would personally travel to Burma to make the arrangements and ensure that the gift was well executed. The formation of good business networks requires careful research.

In 1896, Trench Gascoigne had published some images by the photographer Felix Beato in 'Among Pagodas and Fair Ladies' and, the following year, Mrs. Ernest Hart's 'Picturesque Burma' included more, while George W. Bird in his 'Wanderings in Burma' not only presented thirty-five credited photographs but published a long description of Beato's businesses and recommended visitors to come by his shop.

By that time, Beato's photographs had come to represent the very image of Burma which the rest of the world would retain for decades to come.

As his business developed, with branches in Rangoon, Mandalay, Colombo and London, he also acquired the Photographic Art Gallery in Mandalay in 1903, another photographic studio. In his old age, Beato had become an important business force in Colonial Burma, involved in many enterprises from electric works to life insurance and mining - but I digress.

Felix Beato (1832 – 1909) was the 'go-to' person for anyone searching for local treasures or wanting to commission pieces. For a consideration, he was able to orientate Ulrich by recommending a workshop that had all the requisite skills of carpentry, thayo decoration, lacquer work, glass inlay and gilding. Less developed were their metalwork skills and so Ulrich had made a point of taking hinges and locks from their own company to add the finishing touches to the box. These could also be used for promotional purposes along with the knives, razors and blades which would be the real money spinners.

The chosen workshop was highly skilled in the production of boxes for use in the country's many temples. This was a lucrative business because the per tenancies of the temples were frequently replaced as soon as some deterioration was noticed. The containers of incense and offerings were handled and so they quickly became shabby and therefore disrespectful to the subject of veneration. Boxes containing scriptures had longer lifetimes because they were considered purely decorative and were less handled. Time, rats and insects were their enemies although the insects less so now that most important boxes were being made of teak. This remarkable timber was quickly adopted by the British for all ship's decking. Its resistance to salt water was a natural gift as were the elephants seemingly designed to haul the logs out of the jungle. The distinctive leathery fragrance of Tectona grandis is instantly recognizable to seafarers.

Beato had made a fortune visiting temples and convincing the abbot that his gilded statues, altars and boxes were due for replacement which he was happy to supply. His profit came from selling the distressed originals, complete with the antique patina of sanctity, to tourists and visitors who had an insatiable appetite for antiques along with the deep pockets necessary to acquire them. This had enabled him to set up his photographic studio in Mandalay soon followed by a successful curiosity and antiques dealership in 1894.

The workshop recommended to Ulrich was that of Hsaya Chin. His workshop produced many pieces for the royal household and so was familiar with their tastes and requirements. Young Kaufmann only needed to specify the size, the need for a lock and that it should be gilded, a requirement that generally didn't need to be articulated in a country awash with gold leaf. Chin was a smart businessman and made three suggestions that would add to the cost but enhance the sumptuous appearance of the box. The first was that the box should be fully gilded with 24Kt gold leaf of a slightly thicker gauge than normal. The second was the addition of splayed feet to the box which would give it a more impressive appearance and (incidentally) create additional surface to receive gold. The third was the extra use of glass inlay.

At that time, the use of glass colored with reflective backing was all the rage in Mandalay and, when used in conjunction with 3-D mouldings made from thayo, (a kind of resinous clay) distinguished the Mandalay wares from all others made in Burma at that time. But glass inlay was tedious and time consuming to carry out. First, the small spangles had to be cut out of larger sheets by hand so the smaller the pieces became the more effort was required in their preparation. A useful economy was to use them sparingly and when placed in lines on the gilded surface they would be spaced appropriately. However, for this particular commission, Chin recommended that very small spangles be used and that they should form unbroken lines. The finished effect must be seen by candlelight to appreciate the result of the extra work. The light seems to dance over the surface imparting an even more luxurious appearance to the gold.

Mr. Chin also recommended against the use of any religious motifs. These could occasionally be contentious and so neutral decorative designs with a geometrical bias would be more acceptable.

Top detail showing colored spangles set into gilded lacquer (thayo).

Unusually, the body of the box would be made of two walls of teak for added strength and finished with a layer of good red lacquer made from lacquer sap combined with expensive cinnabar. The mixture known in Burma as hinthabada. All these proposals were acceptable to Kaufmann who studied the impressed stamp on the lock as he handed it over. If the trip proved successful, his father promised that the stamp would henceforth have the addition, '& Sohne' following the Kaufmann name but that lay in the future.

The British, on account of their political and military aspirations had as yet failed to achieve the trade deals so earnestly sought by other European countries such as France and Germany.

The plan and gift organized by the Kaufmanns proved successful and lucrative business followed. Stability and a calm trading climate were short lived. An occasion for colonial intervention was furnished by the case of the British-owned Bombay-Burmah Trading Corporation, which extracted teak from the Ningyan forest in Upper Burma. When Thibaw charged it with cheating the government, demanding a fine of £100,000, the Indian viceroy, Lord Dufferin, sent an ultimatum to Mandalay in October 1885 demanding a reconsideration of the case. Thibaw ignored the ultimatum so precipitating the Third Anglo-Burmese War in November 1885 resulting in total annexation of Burma. On Nov. 14, 1885, the British invaded Upper Burma, capturing Mandalay two weeks later. The royal palace was looted, Thibaw was deposed and exiled to India 24 hours after the British entered Mandalay where he remained until his death in 1916. As part of the spoils of war, the box found its way to England along with many other colonial treasures.

Eventually it made its way to New York where it was acquired by the present owner 130 years after its manufacture. Only then, during routine conservation, was the name of the original locksmith discovered and the history of the box reconstructed. It was fully expected that the lock would be of British manufacture but careful removal of the original lacquer obscuring the Kaufmann stamp finally shone a light on a difficult period in Burma's history just prior to British domination of that gentle land of gold and temples.

The Kaufmann stamp embossed into the lock was hidden by lacquer for 130 years.

8.JAPAN

THE WAR HERO'S Box 1895

When Dr Harry Morton Trafford Jr passed away peacefully on November 17, 2015 at the age of 97, memories of a life well fought and lived began to fade. Twelve years earlier, in deference to his wife, Harry had moved from Miami to Andrews, NC.

Ever since Harry Trafford was initiated into the Ching Tang Fraternity in 1936, he had a fascination with the orient, particularly China and Japan. From school he enlisted in the 2nd Armored Division of the army and participated in the amphibious invasions of North Africa, Sicily and Normandy during WW11. He was seriously injured in Belgium when the Germans attacked in the Battle of the Bulge. It took a year to recover from his injuries but then he returned to active duty before rising to the rank of Commanding Officer of the 336 Field Battalion. Just as he was preparing to be shipped out to Korea in 1953 that war ended but he decided to go anyway to participate in the peace efforts. The drive for travel and adventure was strong.

At that time, there weren't many Japanese still living in Korea as Japanese imperial rule in Korea had ended in 1945 along with the rest of Japan's dreams of empire. Those dreams had ended in cloud of radioactive smoke. Some dreams come true but many more are dashed and as yet no foolproof way has been discovered to predict the winners from the losers. Young Harry was a devout Christian and, unlike many who profess the teaching of the carpenter's son, Harry genuinely had sympathy for the oppressed, the dejected and the broken spirited.

He was drawn to the young soldier who appeared in the church he was attending one evening. Although in American military uniform he appeared to be Japanese.

Takuya Mimura was Japanese American and deployed with the Allied Translator and Interpreter Section (ATIS), then called the 500th MIS Support Group, Far East. He found himself serving as a linguist. He had served on the battlefront, working as an interrogator of Korean POWs, using his Japanese language skills. Many Japanese American soldiers served bravely in the Korean War.

After the war, some continued to serve in various roles worldwide, some moving on to the conflict in Vietnam. Others returned to the United States to restart their lives. Most would return to America, some continued their military careers, many others would quietly slip back into everyday life with little recognition of what they had accomplished during the war. Apart from both being Christians, Harry and Yoshi had in common the uncertainty of what meaning life had for them and where they would call 'home'.

In youth, the excitement of foreign places, sounds, smells and experiences drowns out any thoughts of being settled. It is easier to make friends when abroad. When transplanted to a society different from that of one's adolescence, people unwittingly assume the mantle of the exotic. Interest and curiosity make opening conversation much easier. Speaking to strangers is easy as is being approached by others. At 'home' one is simply part of the scenery, an almost invisible piece of furniture but out of context, one assumes the mantle of the intriguing, the unusual, the rare and, by association, the desirable.

Harry and Takuya spoke often of their background and travels. If there were any thoughts of marrying, settling down and raising families, they went unspoken. Life was lived in the moment. Every day brought opportunities, good and bad, and personal immortality was assumed even though the recent wartime experiences of both proved that pain and suffering were realities but they were the fates of others.

Harry's situation forced him to return to US after a few months but Yoshi was a freer spirit unable to decide if his path lay east or west. Either would be OK although neither beckoned strongly enough to overcome the inertia which kept him where he was, in Korea, enjoying the here and now. But on still nights when the yesterdays outnumber the tomorrows, a wistful nostalgia intrudes. Not the kind that fondly recalls a childhood birthday treat or the laugh of a distant friend, but a longing to pass and leave one's remains in a faraway place. A questioning if there is still time to relocate to the dream place where a plot will be forever baptized anew.

Harry would never know Takuya's destiny. He often speculated on it when he mused over the box Takuya gave him as a parting gift. Its condition was poor; a backpack was not a suitable method of conveyance but it had been remarkable once and would be again when restored to its original condition.

It was made of a smooth and fragrant wood, possibly cedar, juniper or Japanese cypress. Parts were decorated with urushi lacquer but the overwhelming decoration consisted of yosegi veneer.

The box was an exquisite and diminutive expression of the traditional craft technique, "Hakone Yosegi Zaiku", Yosegi zaiku is a technique of creating patterns by joining wood together. "Yosegi" means "combined wood", "Zaiku" means an intricate work and Hakone is the birthplace of the craft. It is located to the west of Tokyo and enjoys spectacular views of Mt Fuji, weather and clouds permitting.

The traditional craft "Hakone Yosegi zaiku" is produced in Hakone and Odawara areas where Yoshi's father originated. The beginning of Yosegi zaiku dates back to about 200 earlier. Nihei Ishikawa, who was born in Hakone, learned the technique of Yosegi zaiku in Shizuoka Prefecture. He began as an apprentice to a master carpenter in the late edo period. its application was for the production of elaborate puzzle boxes used to convey messages between feuding samurai. Such boxes perfectly combine beauty and functionality in typical Japanese style.

Yosegi zaiku became rooted in the area of Hakone, because it was rich in nature and had various trees in the wild in those days. Those trees provided the different colored woods which created contrasts allowing the 100 traditional patterns to be created. All of these are made with wood in their natural color. In spirit, this is similar to Tunbridge ware developed as a decorative technique in England. In both traditions, the vibrant colors, including white, yellow, vermilion and green, are all the natural shades of the wood itself, and not added colors. Trees vary in softness and color depending on the type of tree, the place where they grow in the wild, and the age.

Red…chinese quince, rosewood, zelkova.

White…dogwood, Ilex macropoda, camphor tree.

Dark brown…walnut tree, Japanese pagoda tree, zelkova.

Green…magnolia, Japanese ash.

Yellow…lacquer tree, wax tree.

Black…aged Katsura tree (Cercidiphyllum japonicum).

Only artisans who understand the strengths and weaknesses of each tree can make tasteful and beautiful yosegi zaiku marquetry. The process of gluing together sticks of contrasting colors then cutting thin slices to use as veneers is remarkably similar in principle to the Persian technique of khatam kari aka sadeli when practiced in India. The final appearance, however, is unique to Japan.

Timbers of different colors are cut into oblong rods of desired sections and glued together. Their shaved cross sections are harvested by a skilled woodworker using a razor-sharp plane operating in the 'pull' mode rather than being pushed in western style. Thus emerges the artful and crafty combination of woods to decorate wood. Pieces cut with tolerances of a thousandths of an inch form the notes which, when assembled, form a sonata of surpassing beauty.

In most examples of Hakone zaiku, the pieces are simply juxtaposed but for Takuya's box, the maker isolated each piece with a thin line of black wood to separate it from its neighbors. This has the effect of highlighting the drama of the design by framing each little artistic element thus preventing it from getting lost in the confusion. To continue the musical analogy, these are the barlines separating each musical phrase. Individuals are understood by association with neighbors but should not touch them. That would be a bridge too far.

No screws, nails or even dovetails. The box is held together by the simple gluing of joins fashioned so accurately that no glue line is visible. It is as though the wood elements meld together. The reassembly of the pieces to correct a shoddy restoration, testifies to the precision with which each constructional piece is cut. An error of a fraction of a millimeter in joining two pieces, say, a wall to the base, throws the whole piece out resulting in awkward gaps and a door that won't slide properly.

When the front panel is slid open, three small drawers are revealed. Each has a unique pull in the shape of a fruit with auspicious meaning.

Persimmon -- these fruits are a symbol of longevity and good luck. Some Japanese families also gift them to friends and family as a gesture of goodwill.

Pomegranate - Symbol of fertility due to its many seeds

Double gourd - In Japan, the gourd has several meanings: longevity and fecundity. It also symbolizes "plenty."'

The body of the box had become warped with time and its little sliding lid no longer functioned smoothly. During the restoration process seeking to reverse the vicissitudes of time and travel, complete disassembly was required so the necessary remedial actions could be taken.

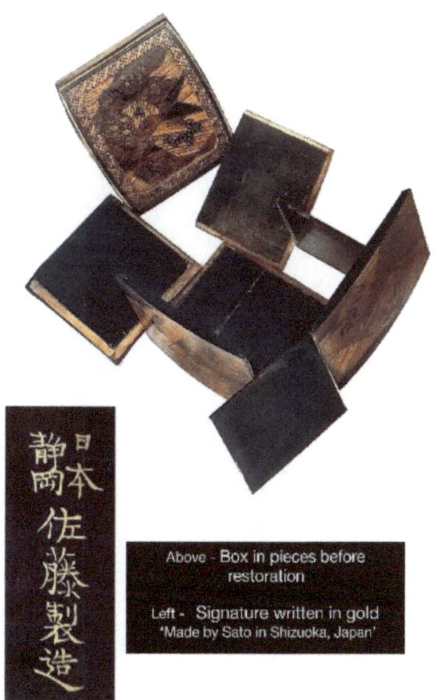

Above - Box in pieces before restoration

Left - Signature written in gold 'Made by Sato in Shizuoka, Japan'

Depicted in gold lacquer across all three drawers, is the poignant image of a heated teapot with two small cups awaiting the arrival of a friend to share. Perhaps when the cherry blooms again.

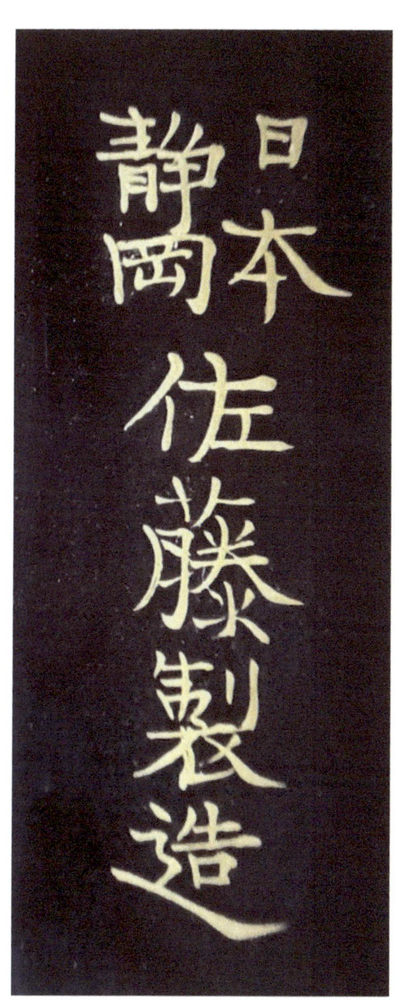

The box's maker is disclosed in gold, eternal symbol of luxury. When translated, the words read:

'Made by Sato in Shizuoka, Japan.

K. Sato worked in Shizuoka prefecture at the end of the Meiji period c. 1890. Occasionally he was commissioned to make larger pieces of furniture for export and, in that case, his name would be written in English. But this box was commissioned locally and never expected to travel but, as Takuya found, the future is mysteriously unpredictable.

Today, Harry and Takuya are gone and SATO SANGYO CO., LTD. today makes office equipment!

I know of what I speak, dear reader. I am Anglo Scottish who spent formative years in South America now living in Pennsylvania holding the Japanese box gifted to an American in Korea.

Purple heather or dreaming spires. Andean mountains or Egyptian sands. All the memories of laughs, loves and life are now shadow plays with departed actors. The stages are quiet now and the backdrops fading, visible but quiet; frozen in the memory.

Perhaps we cannot choose the ending; maybe it is chosen. Maybe the where is less important than the who.

The box will outlive us all.

'So long as men can breathe or eyes can see,
so long lives this and this gives life to thee'.

Shakespeare, Sonnet #18

Post Script-

The boxes described in these short stories are all taken from the author's collection of historical boxes. Others will be the subjects of more stories to be written in due course, time and inspiration permitting.

For further details regarding any of these or other historical boxes, feel free to contact the author directly at;

glennpwood@yahoo.com

Coming soon

Who is Glenn Wood? Enquiring minds want to know.

He spent a childhood in the suburban Victorian sanctuary of Southport hidden in Lancashire away from the Satanic mills of Manchester and commercial energy of Liverpool.
He received spiritual awakening and guidance in the ancient universities of St Andrews in Scotland and Oxford in England. Philosophy and Chemistry make great bedfellows.

Formative experiences were derived from overwhelming interior spaces created in stone by Shah Jahan in Agra, pharaoh Khufu in Giza and the cathedral builders of northern Europe from Canterbury to Cordoba.

He has ears that heard stories of hardship and triumph from his Scottish grandma and the sounds of Aymara panpipes, charangos and guitarras in Bolivia where he played classical violin in that country's

National Symphony Orchestra, breathless in the high Andes.

He has witnessed the ruins of civilizations crushed in Mexico and Peru by zealots from Spain. Also been awakened by the munching of llamas breakfasting on grass in the ruins of Machu Picchu.

He spent a career studying how light interacts with matter to produce Autumn's golden colors and the ghostly specters we call holograms, ethereal yet visible but untouchable like the ghosts that populate this book. They travel briefly through time reversed, telling their stories through tangible relics of their past. Stories as transient as the chords of a symphony or the flavors of a fondly remembered dish.

His feet walked China's Great Wall in the north and the terracotta warriors' tomb of Xi'an in the south.

To Borobudur in Indonesia and the slums of Bombay.

Throughout history, most have lived, loved, cried and died without ever leaving their villages.

But these tales are some of the whispered memories of times past, not of Proust but of my life well lived and filled with the world's riches offered to those with the means to travel and the sense to accept them.

He speaks English and Spanish fluently, Italian, French and Portuguese less well. He has tried to learn German, Chinese, Arabic, Japanese and Russian and now, with the aid of Google translator, can navigate all languages though none better than through the universal language of music.